CLOSE-UP

FOOD

BROWN
BEAR
BOOKS

Published by Brown Bear Books Limited

An imprint of
The Brown Reference Group plc
68 Topstone Road
Redding
Connecticut
06896
USA
www.brownreference.com

ISBN: 978-1-93383-412-2

Authors: John Woodward and Leon Gray
Designer: Lynne Lennon
Picture Researcher: Rupert Palmer
Managing Editor: Bridget Giles
Production Director: Alastair Gourlay
Children's Publisher: Anne O'Daly

Picture credits
Front cover: Science Photo Library; David Scharf
Title page: Photos.com
Photos.com: 25; Science Photo Library: Biophotos Associates 17; Dr. Jeremy Burgess 11, 15; CNRI 27; Chris Kanpton 7; Sidney Moulds 19; David Scharf 23; SCIMAT 21; Dr. Linda Stannard; UCT 29; Andrew Syred 9, 13; Steve Tatlor 5.

Library of Congress Cataloging-in-Publication Data

Food.

    p. cm. – (Close-up)

  Includes index.

  ISBN-13: 978-1-933834-12-2 (alk. paper)

  1. Food–Juvenile literature. 2. Nutrition–Juvenile literature. 3. Food contamination–Juvenile literature. I. Title. II. Series.

  TX533.F66 2007

  641.3–dc22

2006103050

Printed in China
9 8 7 6 5 4 3 2 1

Contents

High Fiber

Vegetables, such as broccoli, carrots, and potatoes, come from plants. Plants are made of millions and millions of cells. Each cell is surrounded by a wall of cellulose. The cellulose makes the cell stiff and tough. It gives the plant its strength.

Fiber food

The cellulose in plants is also known as fiber. Some animals break down fiber and turn it into energy. People cannot do this, so fiber has no food value. However, it is still good to eat fiber. Fiber helps push food through the body. It also stops the body from taking in too much fat from our food.

Slimming Diet

If you ate grass all the time, you would use up more energy eating it than you would get from it. The more grass you ate, the thinner you would get.

Broccoli is a mass of tiny flower buds. You can grow broccoli plants in the backyard. If you leave the broccoli to grow, the buds burst open in a show of yellow flowers.

Fungus Among Us

The mushrooms we eat grow in the soil like plants. But mushrooms grow in a different way than plants do. Plants take energy from the Sun and use it to make their own food. Mushrooms eat the rotting remains of dead animals and plants. They feed on the dead bodies and grow under the soil.

Fatal Fungi

Some mushrooms look like the mushrooms we eat. But they can make you sick and may even kill you. These deadly mushrooms contain chemicals that harm the body. Some deadly mushrooms have bright colors that warn animals not to eat them. Never eat any mushrooms you find in the wild.

Help or harm

The mushrooms we eat are called fungi. There are many different kinds of fungi. Some are helpful to people. Bakers use a fungus called yeast to make bread. Other fungi are harmful. They can cause diseases.

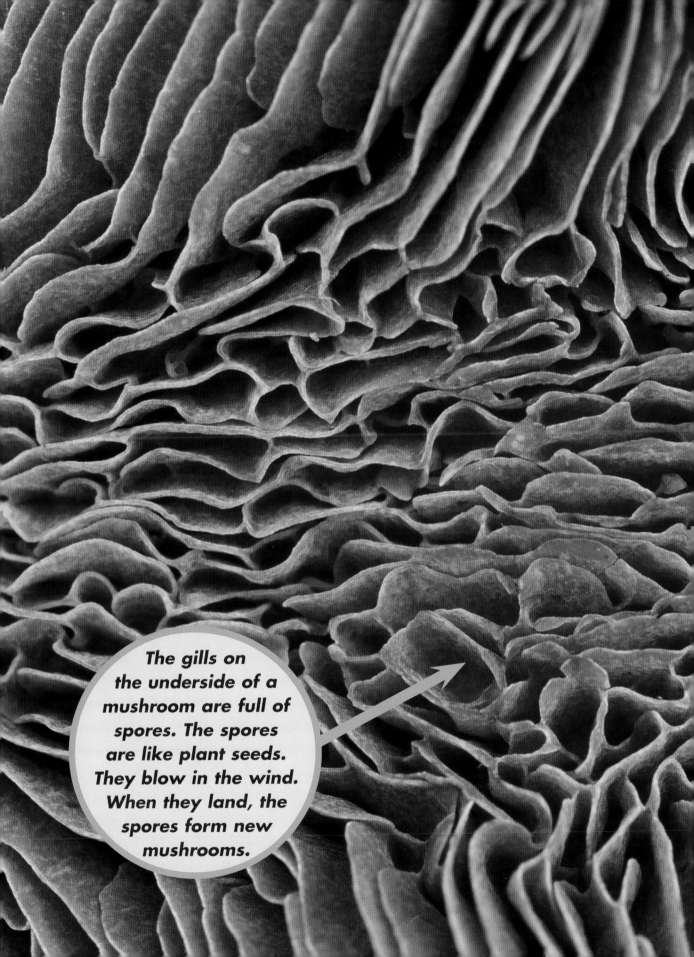

The gills on the underside of a mushroom are full of spores. The spores are like plant seeds. They blow in the wind. When they land, the spores form new mushrooms.

Hot Potatoes

A potato chip is a thin slice of potato that has been fried in hot oil. Potatoes grow under the soil. They are masses of plant cells. The cells in a potato are full of starch. Starch is a carbohydrate, which means it is made up of carbon, hydrogen, and oxygen.

Full of fat

Carbohydrates are good to eat because they give us energy. But a potato chip is also full of fat because it is fried in oil. People need to eat a small amount of fat to stay healthy. But if you eat too many fatty foods, you will put on weight.

Price of a Slice

Ask an adult to cut a potato into chips. How many chips come from one potato? How many potatoes would you need to make a large bag of chips?

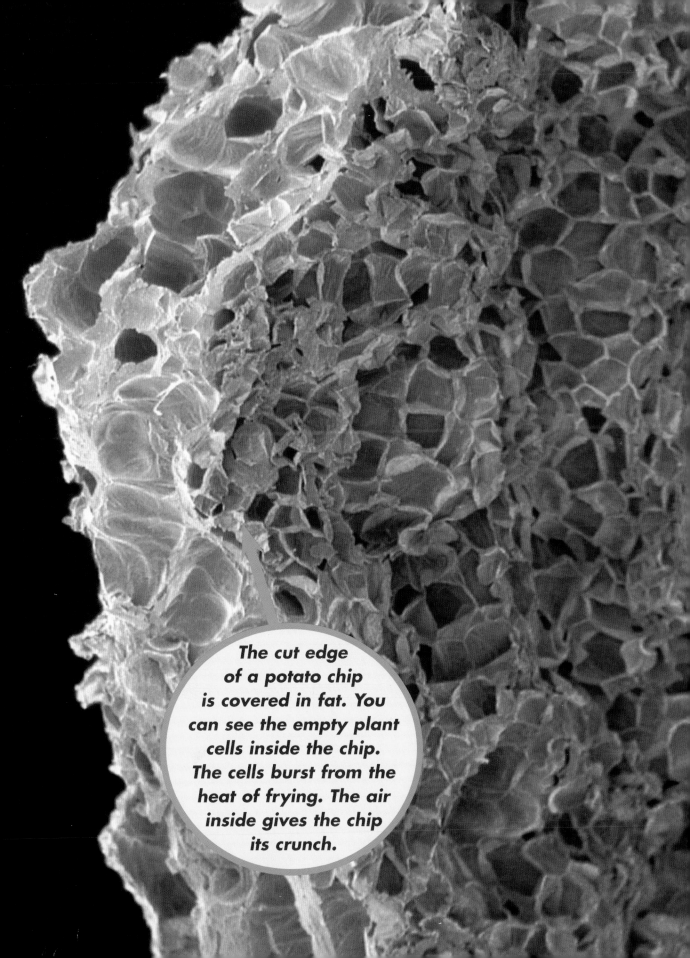

The cut edge of a potato chip is covered in fat. You can see the empty plant cells inside the chip. The cells burst from the heat of frying. The air inside gives the chip its crunch.

Fat Facts

Lots of foods are full of fat. Many plants store fat in nuts and seeds. Some fruits such as avocados are also full of fat. The fats in most plants are unsaturated fats. These fats are usually found as liquids, called oils. Some foods, such as red meat, contain saturated fats. Saturated fats usually occur as solids.

Unhealthy fats

Saturated and unsaturated fats taste the same. But the chemicals that make up the fats join up in different ways. Unsaturated fat is good to eat. But eating too much saturated fat may cause illnesses such as heart disease.

Avocado tree

Remove the big seed from an avocado. Ask an adult to push three toothpicks into the seed. Balance the seed over a glass of water. Fill the glass so the seed just touches the water. In a day or two, you may see a root poke out from the seed. Plant the seed in soil. It could grow into an avocado tree.

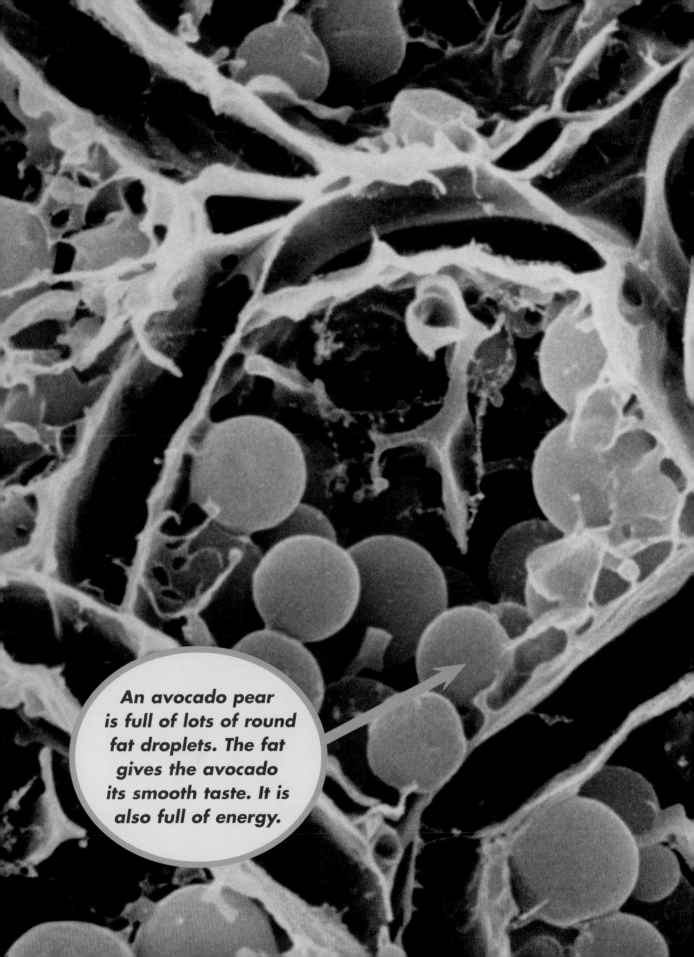

Bread Balloons

To bake a loaf of bread you need flour, water, and a little yeast. First you mix the flour and water. As you add more water, the flour turns into a squidgy lump of dough. Then you add a little yeast. Yeast is a type of fungus. A mushroom is a fungus, too.

Bread bubbles

If you put the dough in a warm place, the yeast produces a gas called carbon dioxide. This gas cannot escape through the springy dough. Instead, it forms tiny bubbles inside the dough. Bread is light and airy because of these trapped bubbles of gas.

Flour Food

When you mix flour and water it becomes sticky. In the past, people used this glue to stick the pages of books together. However, the glue attracted tiny insects called book lice. The books fell apart as the book lice ate the glue.

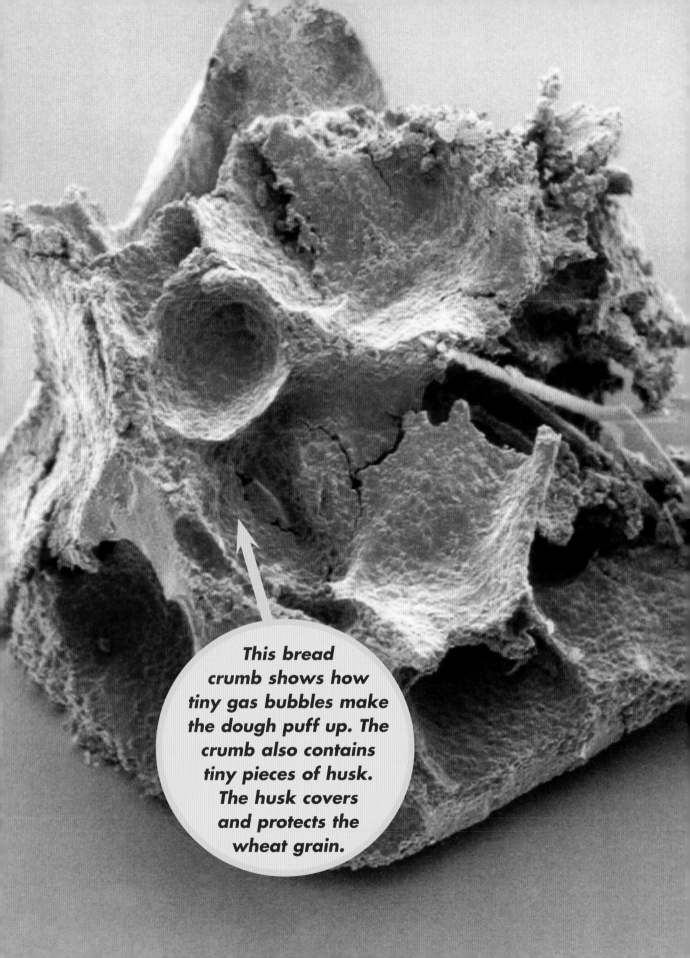

Garlic Glory

During the winter, a garlic plant stores energy in a large bulb buried under the ground. The bulb is made up of lots of cloves of garlic. Each clove is a tight bundle of thick leaves wrapped in a papery skin. There is a lot of energy stored in each clove. The plant uses this energy to grow new leaves and flowers in the spring.

Growing Garlic

Plant a clove of garlic in your backyard in late winter or early spring. The clove is like a seed. It grows into a new garlic plant. When all the leaves turn brown and die in summer, dig up the plant. You should find a new bulb of garlic cloves under the soil. Try cooking a delicious meal with the garlic you have grown.

Garlic is good

The high energy of garlic makes it good to eat. Garlic may keep your heart healthy and stop harmful dieases such as cancer. But most people use garlic to flavor food because it has a strong taste and smell.

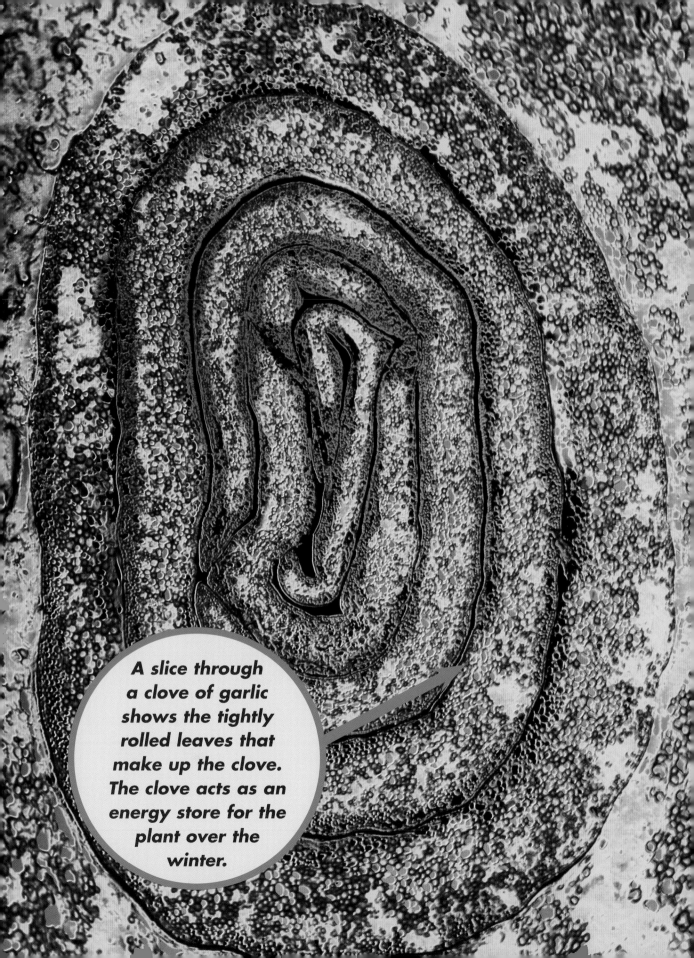

A slice through a clove of garlic shows the tightly rolled leaves that make up the clove. The clove acts as an energy store for the plant over the winter.

Mammals and Milk

Animals called mammals, including people, produce milk to feed their babies. The mother makes the milk inside her body. The baby then sucks on the mother's teat to drink the milk. Milk contains all the goodness a baby needs. It also helps protect the baby from disease.

Dairy products

As adults, most mammals stop drinking milk. But most people drink milk all their lives. We also eat foods made from milk, such as cheese and yogurt. These foods are called dairy products.

Dairy Scare

Babies find it easy to break down milk and turn it into energy. This helps them grow quickly. But some people cannot drink milk or eat dairy products. Part of the milk makes these people feel ill.

The round drops of fat in whole milk are a type of saturated fat. It is not good to eat too much saturated fat. The fat in whole milk may be removed to make skim milk.

Sweet Treats

Sugar has been used to sweeten food for hundreds of years. Sugar is high in energy. If you eat too much sugary food, the extra energy in the food is stored in the body as fat. Too much fat will make you overweight. Sugar is also bad for our health because it rots our teeth.

Sweet to Eat

Food scientists have produced many different types of sweeteners. One sweetener called saccharin is up to five hundred times sweeter than natural sugar. Aspartame is the most popular sweetener in the United States. It is in a wide range of "low-sugar" foods and drinks.

Sweet substitute

Many people now use sweeteners instead of sugar. Sweeteners have a sweet taste but do not make us fat or rot our teeth. Some people think that sweeteners are just as bad for our health. It is probably best to cut down on sweet foods altogether.

Sugar crystals form when the water in a mixture of sugar and water boils away. The sugar particles then line up in a regular pattern called a crystal.

Help and Harm

Fresh food does not stay fresh for long. Left in the heat, fresh milk turns sour in a few hours. Even in a refrigerator, milk only lasts for a few days. But processed milk in the form of a powder can be kept for months. This milk is useful in emergencies, such as when people are starving.

Processing problems

Food processing makes our lives much easier. It allows us to keep food for much longer. But most processed foods are not as healthy as fresh foods. Some may even contain harmful chemicals. It is better to eat fresh food when you can.

Mystery Food

Look at the ingredients on the labels of a few packaged foods. Have you heard of them before? If you are unsure about what you are eating, it is better to buy fresh food and cook it yourself.

These grains of milk powder were made by removing the water from fresh milk. Milk powder is easier to store and lasts for much longer than fresh milk.

Active Yeast

Yeast is a type of fungus, like a mushroom. Most fungi consist of many cells that link up like bricks in a wall. Each cell cannot live without all the other cells in the fungus "wall." A yeast cell is a single "brick" that can live by itself. Yeast is usually found as a mass of single cells. The mass of cells is called a colony.

Yeast at Work

Stir a spoonful of dried yeast into a glass of warm, sugary water. The yeast feeds on the sugar in the water. The sugar gives the yeast the energy it needs to build new cells. As it feeds, the yeast changes the sugar into a liquid called alcohol and a gas called carbon dioxide. You can see the gas bubble up to the surface of the water.

Help and harm

Some yeasts are extremely useful. People use baker's yeast to bake bread and brewer's yeast to brew beer and wine. Other yeasts are harmful to people. They live on our skin or inside our bodies and cause diseases.

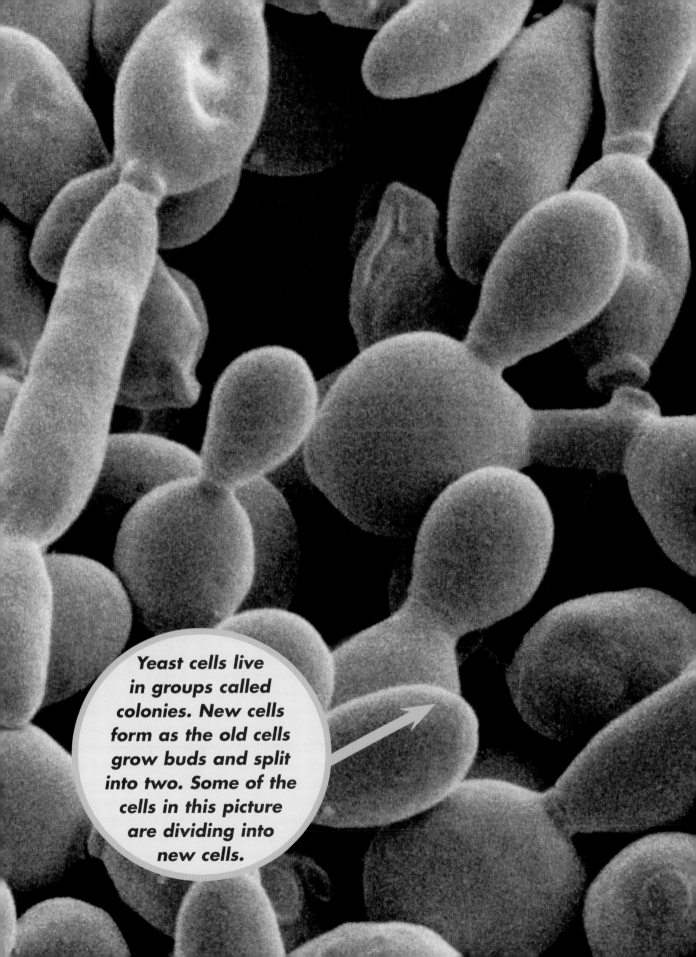

Yeast cells live in groups called colonies. New cells form as the old cells grow buds and split into two. Some of the cells in this picture are dividing into new cells.

Crystal Cubes

Table salt is used to make our food taste better. Table salt contains two main ingredients—sodium and chlorine. The sodium and chlorine link up to form a cube-shaped particle called sodium chloride.

Changing crystals

Crystals of table salt form when the water in a mixture of salt and water boils away. Like the sodium chloride particles, salt forms almost perfect crystal cubes. Most salt does not occur as pure sodium chloride. Other chemicals mixed with the salt change the shape of the crystals.

Essential Salt

Salt is found in every cell in the human body. People cannot survive without salt. Most adults need to eat about 0.1 ounce (3 grams) of salt every day. This replaces the salt we lose in our sweat and urine.

The crystals of pure salt in this picture are almost perfect cubes. The crystal shape changes when the table salt is mixed with other chemicals.

Unwelcome Worm

Some animals, called parasites, live inside the bodies of people and other animals. It is warm and wet inside an animal's body. There is also plenty of food to eat. Many parasites are worms. The biggest is the tapeworm.

Warning Signs

Unless you eat raw beef, it is difficult to pick up a tapeworm parasite. If there is a tapeworm in your body you will eat a lot of food but feel hungry all the time. Over time, you will lose a lot of weight and feel weak. The only way to get rid of a tapeworm parasite is to take special drugs.

Stomach clingers

Young tapeworms grow inside the bodies of cattle. They can get inside the human body when people eat raw or undercooked beef. The tapeworm uses sharp hooks and strong suckers to cling to the stomach. The body of the tapeworm trails behind, often for several feet, soaking up food through its skin.

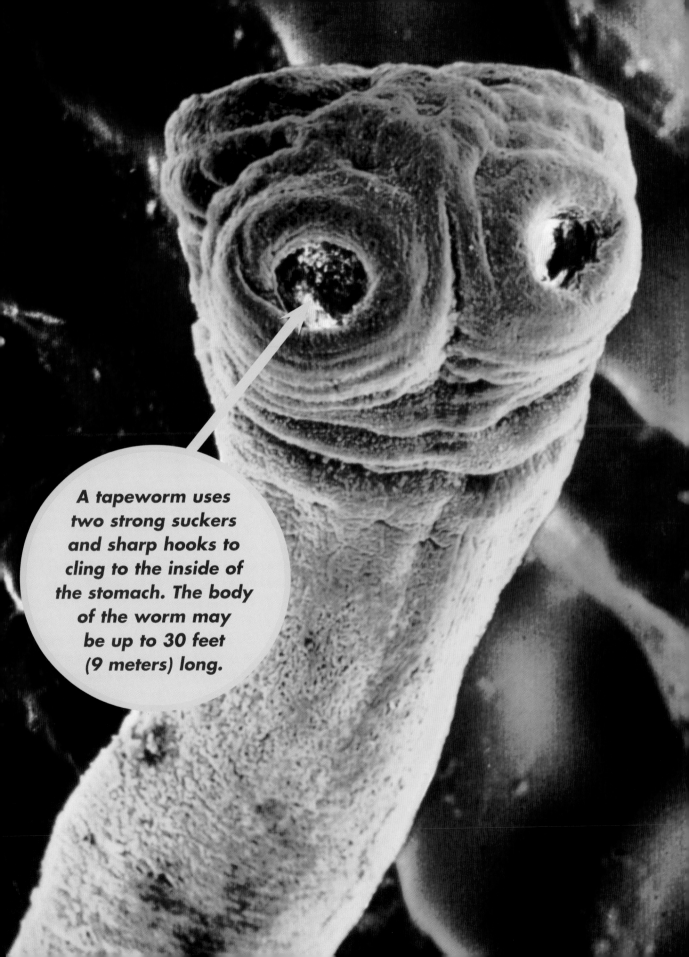

A tapeworm uses two strong suckers and sharp hooks to cling to the inside of the stomach. The body of the worm may be up to 30 feet (9 meters) long.

Poison Food

Cooking can make some foods taste better than raw foods. Heating food also kills tiny creatures called bacteria in the food. Some bacteria in food are harmless. Others are very dangerous.

Harmful bacteria

Salmonella bacteria are extremely dangerous. In the warm and wet insides of the body, *Salmonella* bacteria grow quickly. Some *Salmonella* bacteria cause food poisoning. Others cause serious diseases such as typhoid fever.

Chicken Chores

Most food poisoning is caused by *Salmonella* bacteria in raw chicken. Always wash your hands and the knives and cutting boards after preparing raw chicken. The only way to kill the *Salmonella* bacteria in chicken is by cooking it completely.

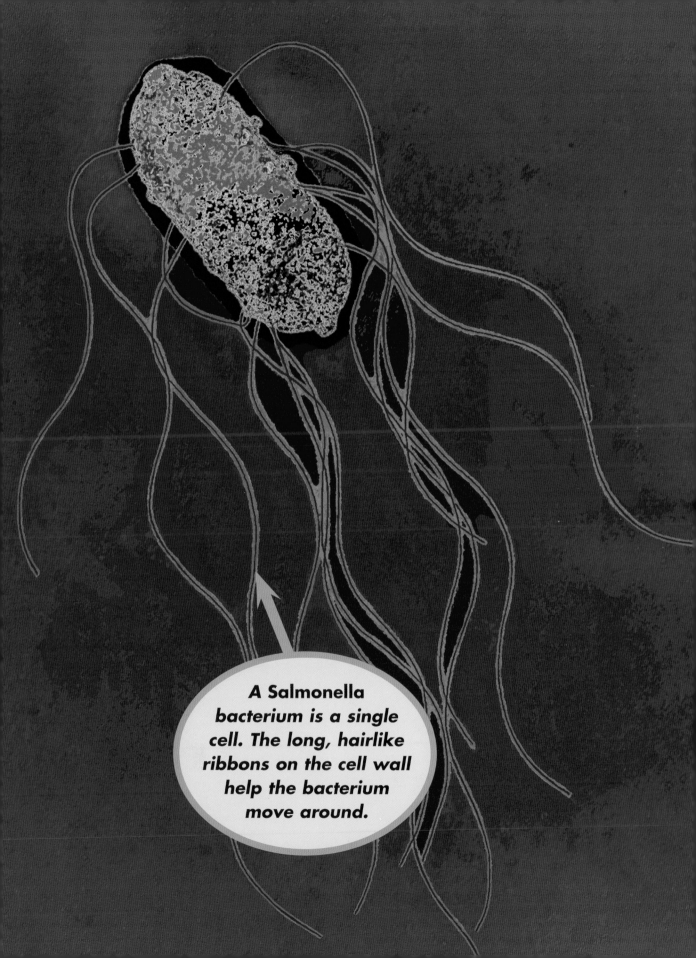

A Salmonella bacterium is a single cell. The long, hairlike ribbons on the cell wall help the bacterium move around.

Glossary

bacteria: tiny creatures made of a single cell; they can be helpful or harmful to people.

carbohydrate: a substance that is made from carbon, hydrogen, and oxygen.

cells: tiny building blocks that make up the bodies of all living creatures.

cellulose: the tough substance that makes up the cell walls of plants.

chemical: any substance found in nature or made by people.

crystal: the regular pattern that is formed by some substances when they become solids.

disease: something that stops the body of a living creature from working properly.

fungus: plantlike creatures that eat the rotting remains of dead animals and plants.

mammal: an animal that has fur and feeds its young with milk from the mother.

parasite: a living creature that lives and feeds on another living creature and causes it harm.

seed: the part of a plant that grows in the soil and becomes a new plant.

spore: the tiny "seed" of a fern or fungus that grows in the soil and becomes a new fern or fungus.

Further Study

Books

Hartzog, Daniel. *Everyday Science Experiments with Food.*
New York: PowerKids Press, 2000.

Kurlansky, Mark, and S. D. Schindler. *The Story of Salt.*
New York: Putnam Juvenile, 2006.

Nye, Bill, Zoehfeld, Kathleen, W., and Bryn, Bernard.
Bill Nye the Science Guy's Great Big Book of Tiny Germs.
New York: Hyperion, 2005.

Taus-Bolstad, Stacy. *From Wheat to Bread.* Minneapolis:
Lerner, 2002.

Ward, Brian R. *Microscopic Life in Your Food.* Mankato,
Minneapolis: Smart Apple Media, 2004.

Web sites

www.mypyramid.gov/kids
Find out about eating healthy foods and keeping fit using
this United States Department of Agriculture web site.

www.fooddetectives.com
The Food Detectives Fight Bac!® web site features fun
games and activities to help you learn about food-borne
diseases and find out how to prevent them.

Index